POWER SERVE

4/15/97

Rob,

Hope you enjoy "Power Serve". I think as much your philosophy on life! May God continue to bless you + your family.

Your friend,

[signature]

Permissions Department
Saltillo Press
7608 Poplar Pike
Germantown, TN 38138
(901) 756-4661
E-Mail: WillifordS@aol.com

Publisher: Steve Williford
Book and Cover Design: Robbin Brent

Library of Congress Cataloging-in-Publication Data

Baggett, Byrd.
    Power Serve: 236 inspiring ideas on servant leadership /
  Byrd Baggett.
        p.   cm.
ISBN 1-890651-00-1

1. Leadership.   I. Title.

Printed on approved acid-free paper

1 2 3 4 5 6 7 8 9 10

236 Inspiring Ideas
on Servant Leadership

Byrd Baggett

Saltillo Press
Germantown, Tennessee

Dedication

Power Serve is dedicated to the many servant leaders who have touched my heart and soul.

A special thanks to my wonderful parents for their unconditional love and support. Mom, you had the heart of a lion and this passion gave me the courage to achieve my dreams. May your beautiful soul continue to shine in God's heaven. Dad, your gentle spirit continues to be a source of peace and encouragement in my life. I love you both and thank God for your powerful presence in my life!

A final tribute to the men and women around the world who are devoting their lives to the most honorable mission of all:

Servant Leadership.

Good luck and Godspeed!

Acknowledgments

The "seed" for a book on servant leadership was planted during the fall of 1996 as a result of my participation in a client's annual meeting. I was asked to talk on the subject of servant leadership to several hundred "Merry Maids" franchise owners at their annual conference in Memphis, Tennessee. The response from the audience was overwhelmingly positive, as several attendees personally thanked me for "touching their hearts." I received several testimonial letters in the days following this event. I would like to share some "magic moments" from two of these letters:

Your presentation on 'servant leadership' struck a responsive chord with our franchise owners. Many in the audience were moved to tears. What a needed reminder that life's greatest satisfaction does not come from making money but serving others!

Byrd, you have a gift for presenting simple, life changing truth in a powerful way. Thanks for sharing from your heart and by your life's example.

Sincerely,

Jeff Fendley
Franchise Development Manager
October 28, 1996

Also:

Byrd,

Although you no doubt have affected many people in the talks you have given, I was deeply moved by your words. My wife, Collins, and I share a vision that one day we will succeed in running our operation without tactics but with love.

As I came to the National Seminar, I felt empty, cynical and in need of some direction for coping with the disappointments associated with a turnover rate of 226%. You have a rare talent that is obviously a gift from God. During your talk, you led me through an emotional ride that kept me on the brink of tears, and you shared your tears in a manner not seen by men in your profession. I have set my goal on a course of personal improvement with the principles of leadership you so strongly represent.

Sincerely,

Tim Chalmers
Franchise Owner
October 11, 1996

This was all the encouragement I needed — *Power Serve* was born!

A special heartfelt thanks to Steve Williford, President of Williford Communications. Steve is a close friend, mentor and one of the most talented individuals in the writing, publishing and editing fields. He was the driving force behind this book. Without his encouragement and support, *Power Serve* would still be a dream.

The creative genius behind *Power Serve* was Robbin Brent. Her obvious talents are only surpassed by her energy, excitement and enthusiasm. Thanks Robbin for putting the pieces together in a beautiful way!

Finally, I must acknowledge the many servant leaders that I have observed during my life. Their habits are the heart beat of *Power Serve*!

Introduction

ervant Leadership. There is not a more powerful combination of words. A dynamic synergy occurs when people serve each other. I have been blessed with opportunities to speak to thousands of people across the country, from minimum wage employees to those who run major corporations. I speak on sales, customer service and many other business related topics, but servant leadership is my favorite.

My books have become worldwide best sellers and I am proud that others want to read what I have to say. But, as I travel and visit with fine people across the country, there remains one constant — People are lonely, confused and frightened about their future.

Why? I believe that people are lost in the high tech whirlwind of change and uncertainty. The downsizing phenomenon has done more damage to loyalty than any other paradigm in the history of corporate America. The reason for such a tragedy must be placed solely on the shoulders of management.

Change is inevitable, no one can intelligently debate this, but we can make a strong case that we have done a miserable job of managing change. Downsizing, or blood-letting, as an associate describes it, has improved (temporarily, I feel) the bottom line but wrecked the lives, self worth, pride and dignity of thousands of employees and their families. History will prove that this insensitive handling of people's hearts and souls will be a major obstacle to healthy organizations.

But, there is good news! The heroes are the few servant leaders who realize the worth of people. Great leaders like Sam Walton, Dave Thomas, Dave Longaberger, William Pollard, Herb Kelleher, Jack Welch, Mary Kay Ash and Bud Hadfield. People who understand the power of love and passion. People who place the well being of employees above the daily value of their stock. These men and women understand the wisdom of serving others and the positive influence that servanthood has on the balance sheet.

My hope is that you benefit from the information contained in **Power Serve**. I feel passionately that servant leadership is the "High Touch" solution to many of our problems in the work place and home place. The #1 goal of this book is that you become a servant to others. If this occurs, thousands of people will achieve their dreams and, most importantly, will understand that there is hope for the future. Good luck and may God bless you on your journey to servant leadership!

—*Byrd Baggett*

Power Serve

Servant leaders do not wander far
from the front line.

Practice random, not programmed,
acts of recognition.

Make sure thoughts are filtered through the heart before they become actions.

Stop, listen and think before you respond.

Do not practice the ready, blame, fire technique.

Time is capital. Invest it wisely.

The greatest gifts will ultimately come to the most generous givers.

Understand the difference between knowledge and wisdom.

When people say it can't be done is most likely the best time to do it.

"I studied the lives of great men and famous women, and I found that the men and women who got to the top were those who did the jobs they had in hand, with everything they had of energy and enthusiasm and hard work." —*Harry S. Truman*

Stay always within the boundaries
where God's love can reach
and bless you.   —*Jude 21*

The greatest affliction of life is
never to be afflicted.

Technology will never replace the true heart and soul of corporations: people.

Avoid stupid controversies.
—*Titus 3:9*

The primary focus of a leader is the development of people.

"The best portion of a good man's life is his little, nameless, unremembered acts of kindness and of love."
—*William Wordsworth*

He climbs highest who helps
another up.

If you want people to improve, let
them overhear the nice things you say
about them to others.

Leaders with high self-esteem are less permissive than those with low self-esteem.

A healthy sense of humor is a necessary ingredient of success.

If all you focus on is winning,
you won't.

Before you can dream,
you must have hope.

"A business is a reflection of the leader. A fish doesn't stink just from the tail, and a company doesn't succeed or fail from the bottom."
—*Gary Feldman*

First and foremost, a good leader serves others.

Provide the sky in which others can soar.

Lead people, not organizations.

Manage yourself, lead others.

"But" — the most destructive word in a leader's vocabulary. *"You did a great job, but ..."*

The abuse of another's self-esteem
is a cardinal sin.

Life's most natural and effective
cosmetic surgery: a smile.

There is nothing in this world more honorable than to help others succeed.

A clear conscience is the trademark of a great servant leader.

People want "High Touch"
not "High Tech."

The #1 want of people — to be
appreciated for a job well done.

Trust, once lost, is almost impossible to regain.

The #1 rule of servant communication: Walk the talk.

"From now on, any definition of a successful life must include serving others."   —*George Bush*

An enthusiastic, positive attitude creates a magical, magnetic field of attraction.

"I don't know what your destiny will be but one thing I do know. The only ones among you who will be really happy are those who have sought and found how to serve."
—*Albert Schweitzer*

One of the wisest acts is to tap into the wisdom of others.

A guaranteed fast track to success: Tap into the collective hearts and souls of your employees.

Spread as much fame as blame.

The team wants to know if their leader will be there when the going gets tough.

Servant leaders cherish the joy of seeing others succeed.

Choose wings over things.

Two essential ingredients for
personal development:
creativity and confidence.

Unconditional trust is the gem of all leadership traits.

Loyalty is earned, not demanded.

"Mental toughness is humility, simplicity, spartanism, and one other … Love. I don't necessarily have to like my associates but as a man, I must love them. Love is loyalty. Love is teamwork. Love respects the dignity of the individual.
Heart and power is the strength of your cooperation."
—*Vince Lombardi*

A true leader will accept nothing but excellence!

A person's productivity will always be in direct proportion to their perceived self worth.

Leaders understand the necessity and value of practice.

A leader's worst sin: to ignore or waste the potential of others.

Managers talk it; leaders walk it.

How many winners have you coached to the victory stand?

Tap into the power of silence.

"The cure for all the ills and wrongs, the cares, the sorrows, and the crimes of humanity all lie in the one word: *love*. It is the divine vitality that everywhere provides and restores life."
—*Lydia Maria Child*

Servant leaders do not allow their flock to be less than they are capable of being.

Help others achieve small daily
personal victories.

Use potential, don't bury it!

"One of the most common problems in our society is unsuccessful people with great potential."
—*Hubie Brown*

Those who get the most out of the least will celebrate the most victories.

If you manage yourself well,
others will follow.

"Everybody can be great ...
Because anybody can serve. You don't
have to have a college degree to serve.
You don't have to make your subject
and verb agree to serve. ... You only
need a heart full of grace, a soul
generated by love."
—*Martin Luther King, Jr.*

Focus more on teaching than preaching.

If you are sensitive to one's wants, they will exceed your expectations.

People

Expect

Openness

Passion

Love

Excellence

Where dignity and respect abound, success occurs.

Your expectations should be in direct proportion to the respect you give others.

If you rule with a stick, you better hope it never breaks.

It is only lonely at the top if you make that choice.

The genius of a leader is
accomplishing extraordinary results
through ordinary people.

Synergy: When *one* serves,
many soar!

Leadership is more natural than management.

If you don't love people, you will never lead them.

"The first and last task of a leader is to keep hope alive — the hope that we can finally find our way through to a better world — despite the day's action, despite our own inertness and shallowness and wavering resolve."
—*John W. Gardner*

A true measure of a leader's effectiveness is in how many they lead versus leave behind.

Be tough minded,
but tender hearted.

Servant leadership is the most
cost effective way of improving
the bottom line.

Philosophy of a servant company:
people working within a system
serving each other and ultimately
the customer.

Focus as much on the employees
as your customers.

In the workplace, you cannot separate the business from the heart.

Pure and simple, people *are* the soul of the firm.

You will receive no greater return on investment than the investment in people.

Leaders *show* the way while managers *control* the way.

"In today's rush and impersonal business climate, it is unusual to find someone doing more than they were expected to do. How about you? What can you give your family, friends and associates? Give them something unexpected, something extra. The results may surprise you."
—*Bud Hadfield*

The one known constant for the future — people!

Search for ideas from everyone, not just a select few.

Managers *hold on* while leaders *let go*.

To enable others to soar, they
must be set free!

People must be happy to be
most productive.

Strength is built from uniqueness,
not sameness.

Hire nice people blessed with
common sense.

Time spent "on the street" teaches
great wisdom.

Most solutions are hidden within
our organizations. We must listen
to find them!

If you don't communicate well internally, you will *never* serve your customers well!

Prospective leaders should be interviewed by those they will ultimately lead.

A true test of a leader's character: Do you remain the same under intense pressure?

Be aware of the emotional and financial costs of turnover.

High turnover is usually the result
of poor leadership.

Leaders understand the power of
perpetual training.

Belief in others gives them the
confidence to be creative and to
take risks.

Effective leaders allow others to tell
them what they need to hear, not
necessarily what they want to hear.

Watch your thoughts;
  they become words.

Watch your words;
  they become actions.

Watch your actions;
  they become habits.

Watch your habits;
  they become character.

Watch your character;
  it becomes your destiny.

—*Frank Outlaw*

Servant leaders understand the power of traditions and celebrations.

You can plan, meet and talk all day but the key is EXECUTION!

Meetings solve little, people do!

Those who are able to tap into the passion of people's hearts will achieve greatness.

Leaders understand and develop the power of the human spirit.

Accept the challenge of turning an ember of possibility into a flaming reality of achievement.

Little acts of recognition have powerful results: handwritten notes of appreciation, roses, candy, etc.

Does your body language contradict your words?

People need to feel what
you are saying.

How you say it is more
important than what you say.

An employee's perception *is* reality.

Are people *hearing* the message you want them to receive?

Servant leaders are like
magicians — they are the magic
in other's lives!

Cowards beat up,
heroes build up!

Leaders are like eagles. They choose to soar in a sky of uncertainty.

Be careful what you say. Once the words leave your mouth, you cannot take them back.

Do not hesitate to apologize and to ask for forgiveness.

"The first responsibility of a leader is to define reality. The last is to say thank you. In between, the leader is a servant." —*Max DePree*

There is nothing more powerful
than the truth.

The past isn't going anywhere,
but you can!

Leadership is more of what you do
versus what you say.

Promote performance, not politics!

Recognition programs
should be rare:

Random

Acts of

Recognition

Everyday

While we have time, let us do good to all men. —*Galatians 6:10*

A simple gift,
when wrapped with passion and love,
becomes a precious treasure.

Hold

On with

Powerful

Expectations

Care as much about the person as
their performance.

Servant leaders understand the
value of daily quiet time.

The truth may sometimes hurt,
but it will always help.

Success will come to those wise
enough to touch the hearts and souls
of their employees.

Perception is much more powerful than reality.

Internal feelings become external actions.

"Reasonable men can differ and remain friends." —*Harold Gould*

An employee's heart and soul is of far greater importance than a daily stock quote.

"If you have ideas and persistence,
you can't lose. Success is within
your reach. So is wealth, which is a
product of being successful. Go for it.
Plant the flag. Light the torch.
Pump yourself up. You can fill in
your own motivational blank.
The fact is, something incredible is
out there waiting to happen."
—*Bud Hadfield*

An organization's full potential is
achieved through the development of
each team member.

Simple things which can change
lives: a smile, a touch, a hug, a note,
a call, a thought, a prayer,
a kind word.

Study the habits of one of the
world's greatest servant leaders:
Mother Teresa.

If your mind says "yes," but your
heart says "no," don't!

If your mind says "yes" and your
heart agrees, do it!

Where a company spends its
time and money is a direct reflection
of its priorities.

Meekness is not weakness.
Meekness is "strength under control."

Sign of great servant leaders:
People seek their wisdom.

If you supply people with the right
information, they will most likely
make the right decision.

There is great joy in taking others
to places they have never been and to
heights they have never dreamed.

Life's greatest teachers —
experience and failure.

"I'll tell you what makes a great manager: A great manager has a knack for making ballplayers think they are better than they think they are. He forces you to have a good opinion of yourself. He lets you know he believes in you. He makes you get more out of yourself. And once you learn how good you really are, you never settle for playing anything less than your very best."
—*Reggie Jackson*

When you speak, people should
feel your passion, energy
and excitement.

One must have the courage to dare
before they can soar.

Understand the true meaning
of help:

Humor

Excellence

Love

Passion

Focus on the pursuit of peace,
not power.

A group of people committed
to a shared vision can accomplish
the impossible.

Learn

Educate

Appreciate

Develop

"It is much easier to be critical
than to be correct."
—*Benjamin Disraeli*

The soul controls the body's actions
— tap into this power.

"I'm okay" is a powerful step in the right direction.

Servant led companies produce great bottom lines.

Addictive behavior can lead to
short-term success but always to
long-term destruction.

Powerful communication exists
where trust abounds.

Greatness is one encouraging
word away.

"We have an MBA program at
Wendy's — Mop Bucket Attitude!"
—*Dave Thomas, Founder, Wendy's*

Understand the power of
"letting go."

"Responsibility is the price
of greatness."
— *Winston Churchill*

Open communication thrives in an
environment of total trust.

There is a beautiful, even magical
and mystical quality, which resounds
from the power of the human touch.

"All true civilization is ninety percent heirlooms and memories — an accumulation of small but precious deposits left by the countless generations that have gone before us."
—*Robert K. Gannon*

To lead others effectively, I must first be at peace with myself.

"What the world really needs is more love and less paperwork."
—*Pearl Bailey*

Beneath the layers of self-doubt
is a masterpiece yearning
to be discovered!

Vast potential is lost by the many
who have been paralyzed by the
fear of failure.

Healthy organizations allow
people to fail.

Leadership is a Sprint:

Special

People

Recognizing

Individually the

Need for

Togetherness

Trust takes so much effort to earn,
so little effort to lose.

"Love is the highest, purest, most
precious of all spiritual things. It will
draw out from men their magnificent
potential." —*Zig Ziglar*

Focus on internal cooperation,
not competition.

Leaders help others find their
purpose in life.

Southwest Airlines' secret weapon:
humor!

People will never be better
(in life's roles) than their perception
of their worth as a human being.

When everyone gives their all,
a victory is achieved!

Power breakfast: positive words
and positive thoughts.

Be grateful when you win;
and gracious when you lose.

"No one of us is more important
than the rest of us."
—*Ray Kroc, Founder, McDonalds*

Your belief can erase another's
self-doubt.

The gift of hope will open your eyes
to previously unseen possibilities
and opportunities.

"Bury your ego. Don't be the star.
Be the star maker!"
—*Bud Hadfield*

If you know the right questions, you
will ultimately gain the right answers.

"Sow" your way to success:

Show up

On time

With a positive attitude

Look for the magic moments.

"Advice is not disliked because it is advice, but because so few people know how to give it." —*Leigh Hunt*

"One can never consent to creep when one feels an impulse to soar."

—*Helen Keller*

Great communicators are great listeners.

"Man is the most extraordinary computer of all."
— John F. Kennedy

Honor others and they will be honorable in their actions toward you.

Take "care" of yourself:

Choices — we make

Attitude — we cultivate

Responsibilities — we accept

Excellence — in all we do

Help others realize that they are
"The Power of One."

Talk less, lead more.

A major casualty of corporate downsizing: the loss of loyalty.

Servant leaders allow others' lights to shine.

Choose intimacy over intimidation.

No trust, no communication.

Please Help Me

Please come into my life —
but don't try to take over.

Please help me to think —
but don't try to think for me.

Please help me to find a
better way —
but don't expect me to do it
your way.

Please help me — even if
I'm wrong.

Help me to stand again —
but don't carry me.

Please help me to move
forward again even if we
move forward in different
directions.

And — last of all —

If you can't help me to be
what I want to be,
then please don't hurt me
by trying to make me
what you expect me to be.

—*Bud Hadfield*

Recommended Reading on
"Servant Leadership"

Lincoln on Leadership   Donald T. Phillips
Warner Books

The Soul of the Firm   C. William Pollard
Harper Business

Leadership is an Art   Max DePree
Dell Publishing

On Becoming a   Robert K. Greenleaf
Servant Leader   Jossey-Bass Publishers

Nuts! The Story of   Kevin & Jackie Freiberg
Southwest Airlines   Bard Press

Well Done!   Dave Thomas
Harper Collins

Wealth Within Reach   Bud Hadfield
Cypress Publishing

Made in America   Sam Walton
Bantam Books

The Customer Comes   Hal F. Rosenbluth
Second   William Morrow & Co.

You Can Have It All   Mary Kay Ash
Prima Publishing

The Life of Jesus   The Holy Bible
Christ